Purple

by Maria Johnson
illustrated by Susan Lexa

Core Decodable 53

McGraw Hill Education

Bothell, WA • Chicago, IL • Columbus, OH • New York, NY

MHEonline.com

Send all inquiries to:
McGraw-Hill Education
8787 Orion Place
Columbus, OH 43240

ISBN: 978-0-02-145867-7
MHID: 0-02-145867-7

Printed in Canada.

9 10 11 12 KOD 24

I am a purple girl.

I have lots of purple things.

I set purple shirts, skirts, and pants in my purple dresser.

I have purple strings
and purple ping pong stuff.

This pitcher has bursts of purple.

I am learning to fill cups.

Mom gets purple plants
from the earth.

No matter where I turn,

I see a blur of purple!